OUR ARABY

J. Smeaton Chase.

A VISTA IN OUR ARABY: MT. SAN JACINTO IN THE
BACKGROUND

OUR ARABY:

PALM SPRINGS

AND THE

THE GARDEN OF THE SUN

BY

J. SMEATON CHASE

———

Illustrated from Photographs by the Author:

WITH A DESCRIPTIVE LIST OF DESERT PLANTS, ETC.

AND

HINTS TO DESERT MOTORISTS:

ALSO

A NEW MAP OF THE REGION
BY THE U. S. GEOLOGICAL SURVEY

———

PRINTED FOR
J. SMEATON CHASE, PALM SPRINGS, CALIFORNIA
BY STAR-NEWS PUBLISHING COMPANY
PASADENA, CALIFORNIA
1920

Republished 1987 by the City of Palm Springs
Board of Library Trustees:
      Betty Beadling
      Rosalyn Bronstein
      Dorothy Kirby
      Beth Olivier
      Lynne West
Republication Project Director: Margaret Roades

Reproduced by Limited Edition Books, A Division of
Horizon House Publishers, 980 E. Tahquitz-McCallum
Way, Palm Springs, California 92262. Printed in
Canada.

Library of Congress Cataloging-in-Publication Data
Chase, J. Smeaton (Joseph Smeaton) b. 1864-1923.
   Our Araby : Palm Springs and the garden of the sun.

   Reprint. Originally published: Pasadena, Calif.: Star-
News Publishing Co., 1920.
   1. Palm Springs Region (Calif.)--Description and
travel.   2. California, Southern--Description and
travel.   3. Desert flora--California--Palm Springs
Region.   4. Desert flora--California, Southern.   5.
Chase, J. Smeaton (Joseph Smeaton), b. 1864--1923--
Journeys--California, Southern.   I. Title.
F869.P18C48   1987   917.94'97   87-18318
ISBN 0-9618724-0-3

FOREWORD TO 1987 EDITION

Almost seventy years ago the prose and photographs of J. Smeaton Chase captured the essence of a unique sleepy desert village, Palm Springs. Now an international resort, the City of Palm Springs is celebrating its golden anniversary. This special fiftieth anniversary republication of *Our Araby: Palm Springs and the Garden of the Sun* is our tribute to the author, to the memory of the village, to generations who never knew the early days and to the lingering charm of our desert community.

Henry Weiss
Palm Springs City Librarian
November 1, 1987

FOREWORD

The late Charles Dudley Warner used to apply to Southern California the term "Our Italy." The territory described in the following pages may certainly be better designated Our Araby; and just as Italy attracts many travellers while Arabia appeals to few, so of the multitude of Californians and California tourists, not many, relatively, are likely to wish to visit the desert: and this is fortunate, for if too much peopled its charm would be lost.

This little book is designed to serve three ends: to invite people of the right kind — not too many — to a region that is meant for the discerning few; to help them while here to enjoy it to the full; and to please them, when they have departed, with recollections of things thought and felt, seen and done, in a tract of country wholly out of the ordinary.

It is hoped that the United States Geological Survey map, supplied in the back of the book, will be found a useful adjunct. Being the only official map yet issued which is complete of the locality dealt with, it meets a definite need. The writer has pleasure in acknowledging the courtesy of the Survey in granting permission to reproduce it, and also to reprint from one of their valuable publications the Hints to Motorists which will be found in the Appendix. He is under obligations also to Professor Joseph Grinnell, of the Museum of Vertebrate Zoölogy of the University of California, for aid in revising the lists of birds and mammals.

CONTENTS

ILLUSTRATIONS

tain's protection and is nourished out of its veins. Two streams of purest water here break from San Jacinto's rocky heart, and make possible this Garden of the Sun, an oasis of pleasant life where Nature had said no life should be except the hard, wild life of her desert children—the plants and animals and Indians of a land of drought.

The village lies at an elevation of 452 feet above sea-level, well toward the foot of the long gradient which runs, smooth as a waterline for league on league, from the summit of San Gorgonio Pass— the gateway and dividing point between California Green and California Gray—down to the great depression where dreams the Salton, that pale, weird Lake-below-the-Sea which came into being (whether for the tenth or hundredth time, who knows?) some fifteen years or so ago when the Colorado River took a fancy to stretch his watery limbs wider in the sun. Bounding this gradient on the north and east runs the level wall of the east-ward extension of San Jacinto's twin mountain, San Bernardino, beyond which wall there is a twin desert, the Mojave. The low narrow scoop, six to ten miles wide, which lies between mountain and mountain, forming a westerly arm of the Colorado Desert, was marked on old maps as the Cahuilla (Ka-we'-ah) Valley, but is now known as the Coachella—a meaningless substitution—and has of late years become famous as a sort of Little Arabia, the source of the earliest of figs, grapes, melons, and asparagus, and especially of those latest and best of horticultural novelties, American-grown dates—whoever has not tried them should lose no time. In its snug elbow at the head of this valley lies our little oasis. I named it unique, and make no apologies for the word.

Walled up thus and all but overhung on the west by the mountain, what kind of landscape is it that spreads north, east, and south from Palm Springs? Strangely, it is one that fascinates by reason of its apparent lack of interest. Looked at in the large, one might even call it dreary, this gray level, treeless and waterless, dotted over with small shrubs and herbage so monotonously alike as to seem machine-made: a wholesale kind of land, all of a piece for leagues at a stretch. Yet this is the land which, if not at first view yet on very short acquaintance, lays hold of you with a charm so deep and strong that it has passed into a catch-phrase—the lure of the desert. Explain it how you may (or give it up for unexplainable, as most people do,) there it undoubtedly is, and none but the most unresponsive of mankind can escape or deny it. Unless you are one of those it will surely "get you," given the chance, and you will find yourself, without knowing how or why, a Companion of the Most Ancient Order of Lovers of the Desert, an Order which far outranks Masonry in age, and might claim Ishmael or Esau, possibly even Nimrod, for its founder.

But I was going to describe a few main features of Palm Springs' outlook. One's attention is at once attracted to two great hills of sand which rise in smooth, dome-like contour a few miles straight ahead, that is, to the east. The larger is, I should guess, five hundred feet or so high, the smaller much less, and both probably represent outlying rocky foothills which, forming obstructions in the path of the wind that blows down the Pass, have in course of ages become submerged under the slow, all-obliterating tide of wind-driven sand. There is something queerly fascinating about these dunes. It may be partly the tricks of light and shade, the chameleon-like play of color which they exhibit; but there is some subtler quality, too. Perhaps there is aroused by the sight of that heap of sand-atoms a geological instinct akin to the sense of infinitude which is raised by the inconceivable figures of astronomy; or perhaps one's sense of curiosity is touched, and subconsciously one wonders what may be hidden under that blanket of sand that defies the eye with its suave, unrevealing outline. However it be, there is something about the great dunes that stamps them strongly on the mind.

Turning to the south the view takes in a sort of bay or backwater—barring the water—of mountain-enclosed desert which may be considered as Palm Springs' private back-yard. Into it open the four cañons which are Palm Springs' pride, viz: Tahquitz, Andreas, Murray, and Palm, the last three being the scenic cream of Our Araby, and notable especially for their remarkable display of the native California palm. It is this tract which it is

A PALM-LOVED POOL IN THE GARDEN OF THE SUN

now proposed to set aside as a National Park, and
a striking addition it will be to the splendid list of
American Wonderlands. This bay, or pocket,
enclosed on three sides by mountains, forms, as it
were, a neat little compendium or miniature of the
greater desert, while Santa Rosa's fine bulk, over-
looking it in the background, gives it even an extra
touch of pictorial completeness. And when, in
winter and spring, the snowy maltese cross shines
on the mountain's forehead, we of Palm Springs
may be excused for indulging the fancy that our
particular bit of desert is distinguished and in a
way hallowed by the sacred emblem.

So wholly distinctive is the locality I speak of
that an effort is needed to realize that so slight a
distance separates it from the familiar landscapes
of the coast regions. As a matter of fact, the differ-
ence between the desert and coast regions takes
effect almost instantaneously, so to speak, at the
summit of the San Gorgonio Pass. Thus it occurs
that from Palm Springs, well out on the desert, to
Riverside and Redlands, the center of California's
finest cultivation, is but a matter of fifty-five miles,
while Pasadena and Los Angeles are but fifty miles
farther away, with the Pacific only a trifle more.
This operates not only to make the journey from
one to the other perfectly easy but also to render
the change spectacular and interesting in a high
degree. To breakfast late at the beach, or "in
town," to lunch leisurely at the Mission Inn at
Riverside (which is strictly the *comme il faut* thing

II. THE VILLAGE

VILLAGE is a pretty word, though ambitious settlements are keen to disclaim the implied rusticity and to graduate into the rank of town or city. Palm Springs has no such aims, and is well content to remain far down the list in census returns. We decline to take part in the race for Improvements, and are (so we feel, anyway) wise enough to know when we are well off. Rural Free Delivery does not entice us: we prefer the daily gathering at the store at mail-time, Indians and whites together, where we can count on catching Miguel or Romualda if we wish to hire a pony or get the washing done. Electric lights? No, thanks: somehow nothing seems to us so homelike for the dinner-table as shaded candles, or for fireside reading a good kerosene lamp: while if we want to call on a neighbor after dark, we find that a lantern sheds light where you need it instead of illuminating mainly the upper air. To us cement sidewalks would be a calamity: we may be dusty, but dust is natural and we prefer it. After all, the pepper- or cottonwood-shaded streets of our Garden of the Sun are really only country lanes, and who wants a country lane cemented? In fact, a little mistake was made when they were named. Cottonwood Row would have been better than Indian Avenue, and

Hot Springs Lane than the commonplace Spring
Street.

The Hot Spring is the outstanding natural feature
of our village, though not so natural as when one
took one's bath in the rickety cabin which antedated
the present solid little bath-house. However, the
Spring itself is as natural, no doubt, as any time
this five or ten thousand years: and you may get as
weird a sensation in taking your bath, and as
healthful a result afterwards, as bygone generations
of Cahuillas have enjoyed. The water, which is just
comfortably hot and contains mineral elements
which render it remarkably curative, comes up
mingled with quantities of very fine sand. You may
bask in the clear water on the surface of the pool,
or, if you want all the fun you can get for your
money, you may lower yourself into the very mouth
of the spring where the mixture comes gurgling up.
This will yield you (especially at night and by
candle-light) a novel and somewhat shuddery
experience, though one absolutely without risk; and
you will come forth with a sense of fitness and fine-
ness all over to which only a patent medicine adver-
tisement writer of high attainments could possibly
do justice.

Our village is bisected by the Reservation line,
which thus makes a geographical division of the
population. Only geographical, though, for, fortunately, there has never been anything but complete
harmony between whites and Indians. Something
more will be said about the Indians later: here I

will only remark that I, for one, could not wish
for better neighbors than our Indians: I should be
pleased, indeed, to feel sure that they could say as
much for us. They are but few in number, forty
or fifty, for the Cahuillas are scattered in small
rancherias over a wide territory. The white population is variable. In winter and spring, when the
"Standing Room Only" sign hangs out, there may
be a total of two hundred or more residents and
visitors (the latter much the more numerous:) in
the hot months residents may number a dozen or
two and visitors there are none. In desert phrase,
the whites have "gone inside" (i. e., to the coast),
an odd turn of speech but one quite appropriate
to the point of view of the man of Big Spaces—
"inside" where one is shut in and boxed up. You
will understand when you have lived a little while
in Our Araby.

For so small a place, the number of people who
have fallen under the charm of Palm Springs, and
their variety of class and kind, are rather surprising.
You would agree as to the latter point if I were to
begin to mention names. Wealth and fashion, as
such, are not much attracted to our village: Palm
Beach, not Palm Springs, is their mark: but among
the fraternity of brains the word has passed about,
and persons of mark are ever finding their way
here, returning again and again, and bringing or
sending others. But then, the importance of persons
of mark in any community is apt to be over-
estimated; the important thing is the general

quality, the average. The average with us is auto-
matically raised by the total absence of any
hooligan element, such as is sometimes in evidence
on the sands of the sea-shore. To that class the
sands of Our Araby do not appeal. On the other
hand, the scientists, writers, painters, musicians,—
in fact, all kinds of people who love quiet, thought-
ful things and whose work or enjoyment lies in
natural instead of artificial fields, come and share
with us the wholesome pleasures and interests that
are inherent in a clean, new, unspoiled bit of this
wonderful old world.

So much for the people. The village itself is a
place of two or three score of unpretentious cottages
scattered along half a dozen palm- and pepper-
shaded streets. We don't run much to lawns and
formal gardens: we live in the desert because we
like it, hence we don't care to shut ourselves away
in little citified enclosures. But the two or three
old places which formed the nucleus of the settle-
ment are bowers of bloom and umbrageous green-
ery. Gray old fig-trees lean out over the sidewalk,
while oranges, dates, grape-fruit, lemons, and trees
of other sorts for fruit or ornament flourish in
tribute to the memory of that wise old Scotsman and
pioneer, Doctor Welwood Murray, who had the
courage to plant and the patience to rear them in
the teeth of horticultural disabilities.

There remain to be mentioned our stores, inns,
school, and church. Of these it is enough to say
that they are well up to what would be expected in

a community such as ours: though one of the inns
might fairly object that this statement comes short
of doing it justice. There are, further, a minute
Public Library, housed in a quaint little hutch of
adobe, which, half a century ago, was the Stage
Station, and a tasteful Rest-house raised as a me-
morial to the old Scottish doctor, named above, who
may fairly be termed the patriarch, well nigh the
founder, of our village.

III. THE INDIANS

TO SAY that the Indians make a main point in the interest of life in our village sounds patronizing, as though the whites were the natural residents and the Indians merely an incidental feature. Of course the reverse is the fact: we are the new-comers: whether "interesting" is the term they would apply to us, or some other, is open to speculation. However, the point is that they are an integral part of the charm of life in Our Araby. Their ways of life and points of view differ from ours enough to give them the attraction of novelty, while their independence and good nature render them congenial as friends and neighbors.

This small band of Indians, a part of the widely-scattered Cahuilla tribe, have lived from time immemorial about the hot spring which gives the Indian village, or *ranchería*, the Spanish name of Agua Caliente, by which the Reservation is still officially known. (There are other places of this name in California, one being the village, formerly a *ranchería* of this same tribe, now generally called Warner's Springs, in San Diego County.) They have long been Christianized, and are numbered among the so-called Mission Indians of California, being cared for, in religious matters, by the Roman Catholic priest stationed at Banning, while administratively they are under the charge of a Govern-

PALM SPRINGS INDIANS AT HOME

ment Agent, whose headquarters are at the town of San Jacinto, on the other side of the mountain.

The reproach of laziness, commonly levelled against Indians, cannot fairly be laid against the Indians of Palm Springs. The men either farm their own little holdings, or work for their white neighbors, or "hire out" on Coachella or Imperial ranches, or, at fruit-picking time, in the prune or almond orchards of the mountains. Some of them are well-to-do, with cattle or alfalfa to sell and horses to rent; besides which they have their patrimony of monumental old fig-trees, scions of the famous Black Mission figs of San Gabriel (and you may have noticed that Palm Springs early figs do not go begging in Los Angeles markets.) Old Marcos is even the proud owner of a few of those original epoch - making date-palms which have opened a new chapter in American horticulture, and his Deglet Nurs have been adjudged by the knowing ones to be second to none.

Of the women, some find time from their own employments to do laundry or other household work in the village, while, fortunately, one or two still practise the old arts and are notable weavers of baskets: a basket by Dolores, wife of Francisco Patencio, who lives down by the *fiesta* house, may well be counted a prize. The making of pottery, sad to say, has ceased: the white man's cheap tinware has driven the artistic but fragile *olla* from the field. But about the sites of vanished Indian homes you will find the ground strewn with frag-

ments, and persons with a nose for relics now and
then make interesting finds of pottery or basket-
ware that was *cached* by long-dead hands in cran-
nies of the rocks. Relic-hunters will find interest
also in the picture-writings which adorn the walls
of near-by caves, and in mortar-holes deeply sunk
in granite boulders, mute witnesses to the back-
breaking labors of departed generations of squaws.

An experience decidedly worth while is yielded
by the *fiesta* which is held in mid-winter of most
years. It is a celebration of remembrance for the
dead, and consists in dancing, in the chanting of
traditional songs of the tribe, in feasting, and in,
finally, the burning of effigies of those who have
passed away since the previous occasion. The
flicker - lighted gloom of the fiesta - house, the
rhythmic manoeuvrings, and the unearthly ardula-
tions that accompany them make a total sufficiently
weird, even without such an adjunct as the eating
of glowing coals from the fire by the medicine-man,
a star performer from a neighboring *rancheria*.
However, all this (which may well seem barbaric
to the reader) must be understood as merely a
belated survival from the dim old days, not by any
means an indication of the ordinary manner of life
of our thoroughly good friends and fellow-villagers,
the Indians of Palm Springs.

IV. AMUSEMENTS

A QUESTION that arises in many persons' minds when one speaks of the desert as a place of any attractiveness is—But what can there be to do there? It is a natural question, too, for to most people the desert signifies only a region of dreariness and horror, a mere waste spot marring the earth's wholesome fertility and beauty. That, however, is a total mistake, one of those conventional delusions that are based only on generations of popular misconception. Only one or two hundred years ago the forests and mountains in which we now delight were thought places of dread and ugliness. People simply hadn't caught the idea; and today, as regards the desert, a few people are just beginning to catch it. Essentially, the desert is Nature in her simplest expression. Has it come to this—that Nature must be spiced up with amusements before we can take pleasure in her? Surely space, quietude, and freedom are fine things: solitude can be magnificent: loneliness need not scare us as if we were lost kittens.

However, as it happens, there are plenty of ways of amusing oneself actively on the desert. The most popular at Palm Springs, undoubtedly, is horseback riding, with or without the adjunct of a picnic. Our Araby is ideal for this sort of thing. The " 'ard 'igh road" is all right for the automobile, which

indeed has fairly claimed it for its own; but the
glory of horseback is the cross-country feature, and
here you have it unalloyed.   The free fenceless
desert stretches before you to the horizon, and
wherever you guide your horse, something new,
strange, or wonderful calls constantly for notice—
new plants and animals, new colors, new shapes,
(perhaps also new thoughts.)   Thus, there are few
Palm Springs mornings that you will not see some
gay party cantering off on the wise Indian ponies
bound for Palm Cañon, or Andreas, or the dunes;
or, maybe, starting more leisurely with saddle-bags
and blanket-rolls on the longer trip down to the
Salton Sea, or into the Morongos, or up the Vandeventer trail to Piñon Flat, or by the Gordon trail
to Idyllwild in the pines.

   To those who are wedded to their ease and their
autos plenty of inviting resources are open.   Good
or practicable roads have been built to several of
the near-by cañons—notably to Palm Cañon, the
favorite—and the main stage-road across the desert
runs through Palm Springs, by which you may go
down the valley as far as you like—or on to New
York, for that matter.   All the valley towns are on
that road—Indio, Coachella, Thermal, Mecca—and
from it one has access to all other roads and may
explore whither and what he will—date-gardens,
fig-groves, the haunts of the earliest grapes, melons,
and asparagus: or may run down beside the Salton
Sea to Imperial Valley, the land of cotton, and "the

line," beyond which lies the land of revolutions, distressful Mexico.

The time has come, too, when flying must be counted in when one thinks of ways and means of amusement or of getting about. There is not, of course, much to be said yet on this score, but it may be remarked that Our Araby is not lagging behind the rest of the world, and already is critical of the pilot who fails to bring his "bus" neatly to earth regardless of cactus and creosote brush. Certainly it would seem that the spacious, level desert is the very model of a natural airdrome, and I look to see aeronauts, professional and amateur, taking Nature's hint and exploiting these advantages. A project is under way for forming the piece of country comprising Palm Cañon and the picturesque localities adjacent thereto into a National Park. I hazard the guess that when this is done provision will be made for air-travel to and about the tract. The American tourist expects to have Nature served up in up-to-date fashion, and Uncle Sam may be trusted to comply.

Under the next heading I outline some of the favorite trips, and the map, it is hoped, will be of use in planning and executing them and suggesting others. There is, so far, a glorious lack of "No Trespassing" signs in Our Araby: our cañons and palm-groves are not yet roped off and adorned with brusque notifications to "Keep Out"; but this state of things cannot be guaranteed to last forever. It

is the age of barbed wire, and even the desert cannot
hope to escape it.

Coming now to the more specific forms of amusement, we have, for those who must be up to date,
"the movies": not the commonplace side of the
great modern pastime, the sitting in a "palace" and
watching the reeling off of pictures on a screen,
but the more exciting first-hand experience of seeing
them made, the thrill of the real thing, flesh and
blood (with paint and powder thrown in.)   In the
last few years Palm Springs has become headquarters, so to speak, for Algeria, Egypt, Arabia,
Palestine, India, Mexico, a good deal of Turkey,
Australia, South America, and sundry other parts
of the globe.   Wondrous are the sights and sounds
the dwellers in Palm Springs are privileged to see
and hear when "the movies are in town": wondrous
the "stars" that then shine in broad daylight on us;
wondrous the cowboys, cavalcades, and caballeros,
the tragedies, the feats of daring, the rescues and
escapes, for which our dunes and cañons provide
the setting.   The quiet village becomes in fact a
movie studio for the time, and the visitor whose
ideal is "Something doing every minute" has then
little reason to pine away with *ennui*.

Moving pictures remind one of the other and, as
a rule, less spectacular kind.   Our Araby, with its
marvelous display of tone and color—tone the
most elusive, color the most unearthly and ethereal
—is a land of enchantment to the painter, and its
fame has spread from one to another until, now,

every winter and spring sees painters of note studying these desert landscapes, so fascinatingly different in their problems of conception and handling from anything that commonly comes in the artist's way. It looks more than likely that by ten or fifteen years from now a school of painters will have made Our Araby their province, just as now there are the Marblehead and Gloucester men in the East and the Newlyn men in England. A forerunner of the group I forecast has already been working for many years with Palm Springs for his headquarters, Mr. Carl Eytel, whose knowledge of his field has been earned, as it were, inch by inch and grain by grain, and whose conscientious work gives a truer rendering of the desert than do sensational canvases of the popular Wild West sort.

The person must be very insensible to natural interests whose curiosity is not aroused by the markedly distinctive vegetable life which the desert offers to the view. From the moment that your train or auto begins to run down-grade on leaving Banning the fact is plain that you are, botanically speaking, in a new world. Gray, the livery of the desert, largely takes the place of green; stunted forms and bizarre shapes notify you that wholly different conditions here reign. Though you may have no leanings toward botany as a science or a hobby you will hardly fail to be interested by the novel objects that surround you, and are likely to find yourself botanizing mildly before you know it, if only to the extent of learning the name of the

cactus that scratched you, or whether it was a
mesquit or a catclaw that tore your clothes. The
cacti alone are "worth the money": the biznaga, for
instance, on close acquaintance is a most engaging
fellow, and seriously, no one should go through life
without interviewing a cholla. A tree that is as
green as grass, yet has no leaves, is worth one's
notice: so is one that is total gray and pricklier
than an armful of hedgehogs, and another that
bears for fruit a neat imitation of a handful of
screws.

But it is when the Great Spring Flower Show
comes on, especially if the rains have come just
right, that our Garden of the Sun shows what it is
capable of botanically. In January one or two
early-waking plants, such as crimson beloperone
and yellow bladder-pod, modestly start the show.
February brings the wild heliotrope and the first
hint of the glory of the verbenas, with clouds of
wild plum in the cañons. March is a steady
crescendo of color, and by mid-April the riot is on
and Flora is emptying her lap over the desert in
cascades of multi-hued bloom. On the levels, pools
of rosy - purple verbenas spread out and run
together into lakes; the mountain slopes, built of
slabs of uncompromising rock, by some magic con-
trive to send out myriads of golden blossoms of the
incense-bush; the cañons turn into mazes and
tangles of flowering rarities that go to the head of
the most experienced botanist. Now is the time to
notice how admirable even a cactus can be when

THE PALMS OF OUR ARABY

Spring gets into its blood; you will hardly match
those silky cups of purple or cerise in greenhouses
of millionaires. The ocotillo, too—where will you
find anything floral that is finer in its way than that
flaming scarlet tongue? It is the desert's own fierce
flower, not on any account to be missed, and well
worth the ride down to Deep Cañon, even if the
ride showed you nothing else worth your notice,
which would be strange indeed.*

There is plenty of interesting matter here, too,
for those to whom animal life appeals. For bird
study, especially, this locality offers exceptional
facilities, for the San Gorgonio Pass is the great
migration highway for a large region, and the Palm
Springs oasis, lying at the foot of the pass, forms a
natural stopping-place for the small travelers. It is
for this reason a favorite station for bird-men, as it
is for naturalists in general. Beetle-men and
butterfly-men, mouse-and-gopher-men, and devotees
of all sorts of zoological ramifications with alarming names spend rapturous days in Our Araby,
collecting, studying, and classifying, with ever in
view the thrilling chance of coming upon something
new—a kangaroo-rat with tail measurement three
millimeters greater than any yet recorded in the
halls of science, or some phenomenal development
of the maxillary arch in a short-nosed pocket-mouse.
Such triumphs have in the past shed lustre upon

---

*Under the heading of *Flora and Fauna* will be found a
  list of all the desert plants likely to be observed, with
  brief descriptions which will aid in identifying them.

zoologically-minded visitors to Palm Springs, which already has a gopher and a ground-squirrel "named for it":—why not again?

Suspicious people, noticing that I have said nothing as to reptiles, may ask "What about the snakes?" Here comes in another popular misconception, the idea that the desert swarms with rattlesnakes, sidewinders, and Gila monsters. The fact is that rattlesnakes are certainly no more numerous on the desert than in the coast or mountain regions: I think on the whole they are fewer here. As for the sidewinder (which is simply the desert's special form of rattlesnake), in several years' experience I have seen but two, one of which was dead when found, while the other was hailed with rejoicing and carried home tenderly in a tomato-can (being needed for photographic purposes), having been an object of daily search for two or three months. The Gila monster, rare at best, is never seen in or near this part of the desert. Ordinary lizards we have in plenty, but they, of course, are wholly harmless, even friendly and amusing. The chuck-walla, with his alligator look, may not be charming, but need cause no alarm to anything bigger than a house-fly.

But this is aside from the matter of the amusements Our Araby offers her visitors. A few words as to sporting possibilities will not come amiss to lovers of rod and gun. Fishing will hardly be looked for on the desert: indeed, the mention of the rod may seem like rather a futile joke. Not quite so, however: for ten miles from Palm Springs is Snow Creek, which comes down from San Jacinto Mountain (debouching about opposite Whitewater Station) and offers fair trout-fishing, as does also the stream in Whitewater Cañon, a few miles away across the valley from Snow Creek. This, I must confess, exhausts the fishing possibilities of Our Araby, unless one is minded to try what can be done with the Salton Sea, where some kinds of coarse fish, principally mullet, are plentiful and seem to give good sport for the gulls and pelicans.

There is more to be said for the gun, however.* Quail are numerous, and give excellent shooting when in season. On the open sandy levels the desert or Gambel quail in good coveys will be found in the vicinity of mesquit thickets: in the cañons the valley species exists in fair numbers: while at higher altitudes the mountain quail appears. Doves may be had anywhere near water by gunners who care to shoot those trustful creatures. A few snipe and duck can be found if one knows where to look for them, but, naturally, such spots are few and far between in Our Araby. The duck-hunter who cares to go so far as to the Salton Sea, however, may expect good sport.

---

*It should be noted that shooting on Indian Reservation land, except by Indians, is strictly prohibited by law. There is a good deal of such land in the neighborhood of Palm Springs besides that upon which the Indian village is situated. Hunters should inform themselves as to the boundaries of Indian land.

Rabbits—jack and cottontail—are a matter of course, though not so much so as in days gone by. Nowadays one may tramp a whole morning in the Palm Springs locality and hardly empty a barrel. Whither the bunnies have gone is rather a mystery. Yet I do know the spot I should make for should an urgent demand for cottontail-stew arise suddenly within me. No, I shall not name the place: that is a little secret between the coyotes and me.

Coyotes and foxes, by-the-by, as also wildcats and mountain-lions, should perhaps be mentioned, but the first-named two are hardly game, while the others are only possibilities of cañon camps. Deer, however, are more than a possibility in some desert localities, though not, of course, on the low open levels. Piñon Flat, reached by the Vandeventer trail, and a good day's trip from Palm Springs, is quite good deer country, and, incidentally, an interesting bit of territory to explore, with or without gun or rifle.

Two other animals that come in the "big game" category may be named, though one of these, the antelope, has passed into history so far as Our Araby is concerned. A few antelope may linger on the stretches of almost untraveled country bordering on the Mexican line, but the chances are slight of this fine creature being ever again reported from the Colorado Desert. The other animal is the mountain-sheep (bighorn) which ranges in all the desert hills and cañons, but is not to be counted for shooting purposes, being strictly protected by law,

with no open season. I said strictly, but must add
—O that it *were* strictly! for it is but too certain
that since the appearance of the automobile (the
worst foe of wild game everywhere) on the desert,
the sheep have fallen victims to illicit shooting to
a terrible extent. Parties of "sports"—the fellows
who bear the same relation to sportsmen that
"gents" do to gentlemen—lolling at ease in high-
powered cars, now invade every part of the desert
where a road leads to some remote mine or pros-
pect, and blaze away at anything that moves, in
mere intoxication of blood-lust: with result of
many a wounded animal, ram or ewe just as it
happens, dragging itself into some haunt inacces-
sible to man, there to lingeringly perish:—the
"sport" making the most of his contemptible feat
by jubilant assertions of "Anyway, I know I hit
him—saw him fall."

Beyond the active amusements, so to speak, which
I have named, there are some immaterial pleasures
to be enjoyed in Our Araby which, I venture to
think, remain long in the memory of those who
come here. It may sound commonplace to talk of
sunset colorings and sunrise panoramas, but anyone who has watched the sunset light on the
Morongos from the rocky point that overlooks our
village will allow that it is a revelation of Nature
in her mood of tenderest loveliness. Nowhere as
on the desert will you experience what I may best
call the spirituality of color, beauty in sunset hues
so extreme that it affects one with a sense of pathos,

even of solemnity, like the innocent blue of child-
hood's eyes. Heavenly is a well-worn term, but
here it comes to one's lips instinctively: such per-
fection in color seems not of earthly kind.

The sky of the desert is well worth studying at
other times than the sunset hour—for instance, at
the moment when the sun comes striding up in
inexpressible magnificence of power. Over this
Garden of the Sun he rises morning after morning
in such splendor as you will never see but in
the desert, for here no mists or earthly exhalations
dim the flashing glory of his first horizontal beams.
It is then that one grasps the true meaning of that
everyday word, the sun, and realizes him at last
for what he is—a Flame, inconceivably vast, in-
effably pure, unutterably terrible.

For those who delight in cloud-form and sky-
scenery, no area of sky that I know approaches in
interest that which stretches from the southern
extension of San Jacinto Mountain eastward to
Santa Rosa Peak. In the rainy season this tract of
air forms the very frontier of the opposing meteoro-
logical forces, where day after day one may watch
the battle between Rain and Drought fought in
fashion more spectacular than one sees it elsewhere.
Some particular interplay of air-currents, combined
with and perhaps arising from the configuration of
the land below, give rise to a remarkable diversity
of cloud conditions. Above Santa Rosa there will
hang for days a vast banner of vapor like the plume
that curls from the lip of a volcano, while in the

upper air beyond and above it, cirrus, stratus, and cumulus merge and evolve in ceaseless manoeuvres. I know of no other such "cloud-compelling peak" as this, on which another admirer and I have ventured to confer the title or degree of *Santa Rosa de las Nubes* (Santa Rosa of the Clouds.)

Other aerial phenomena occur in these desert skies, some of them so unusual that one may suspect one's eyes of playing tricks: as, for instance, I did, one evening when riding from Andreas Cañon soon after sunset. The western sky was hidden from me by the high wall of mountain on my left; but suddenly I saw on my right—that is to say, *in the East* —the well-known effect of radiating beams of light, frequently seen when the sun is at or near the horizon. I reined up and stared: yes, there it was, plain, even vivid. What was up? Had West become East, and East, West? Or couldn't I tell one from the other? These were alarming thoughts, but soon I realized that the desert was up to one of its tricks: what I saw was the sunset *reflected* by the eastern sky.

And then there is the night. It may seem odd to speak of sleep under the head of Amusements, but such sleep as one gets on the desert fairly ranks as enjoyment, so it is much the same. Few people know what night at its best can be. The desert is the place to learn it. Calmness, quietude, restfulness, as a rule very relative terms, here approach the absolute. We speak of balmy sleep, and sometimes think we get it in a bed under a ceiling; but

"THE MOONLIGHT SONATA"
From a painting by Mr. Carl Eytel, Palm Springs

V. TRIPS TO THE CAÑONS AND OTHER NOTABLE POINTS

I T IS NOT possible in this small book to describe in detail the many points of special beauty or interest which lie within the range of Palm Springs. Here, however, are given brief notes regarding the spots most worth visiting, such as will serve to outline their particular features and to explain how they may be reached. In the latter connection, attention is directed to the map which will be found inside the back cover.

For convenience I take them in alphabetical order.

Andreas Cañon is four or five miles south of Palm Springs, on the way and a little to the west of the road to Palm Cañon. A fair automobile road goes right to the cañon-mouth. There are fine cliffs of the palisade sort, some caves with Indian relics, and many palms, one group of which is remarkable. There is a stream of pure mountain water, and some lovely cañon scenery. A divergence may be made on the return trip by taking a trail on the north side of the cañon, which leads up to the Gordon trail and gives a splendid view of the palisade cliffs and the desert: then descending the Gordon trail, which connects with the regular Palm Cañon road. (See Gordon Trail trip.)

Cathedral Cañon is about seven miles southeast of Palm Springs, opening to the west of the main road down the valley. There is a fair automobile road into the cañon, but to reach the narrows a rough walk of two miles further is required, which by most people would not be thought worth while. There are a few palms and sometimes a little water.

Chino Cañon is the wide-mouthed cañon which opens to the west of the main road a mile or two north of Palm Springs. No practicable road runs into the cañon, but a trail (formerly a wagon-road) may be picked out, roughly following the pipe-line. In the neck of the cañon there is a *ciénaga* (marshy meadow) and a fine grove of cottonwoods: also a group of palms beneath which is a warm spring which makes a luxurious natural bathing-place: adjacent is a stream of cold mountain water. Near the point where the cañon narrows to a gorge there is a cave that is worth visiting; and continuing one comes to a cliff of about 5000 feet sheer. Fine views of the desert are obtainable. If the return trip be made by moonlight a weird effect may be observed, produced by the reflected light from the mountains on either side. Time needed, two or three hours each way, as the trail is rough.

The "Coral Reef." This is of course no coral reef nor is it anything like one. It is simply a part of the mountain wall on the southwest side of the Coachella Valley, some twenty-five miles from Palm

Springs and about six miles southwest of the town
of Coachella (the same from Indio.) The old
Indian road to Toro and Martinez passes near the
"reef." The land is here below sea-level, and the
water-line of the ancient sea is plainly marked on
the foot of the mountain. The "coral" is a deposit
of calcium carbonate left by the water. The like-
ness to coral is not really close. There are ranches
in the neighborhood.

Deep Cañon is a main cañon of Santa Rosa
Mountain, reached by following the main road
down the valley for thirteen miles from Palm
Springs, when a road will be found which runs
some distance into the cañon, though not so far as
the narrows, which are five miles up. Botanists
will find this a good piece of country: there are
some splendid palo verdes, cacti are in fine display,
and ocotillos and agaves are numerous. Beyond the
narrows the cañon is rocky and romantic. The
walls are strikingly high and steep, and a few palms
are scattered along the stream.

The Devil's Garden. This is a tract of open
desert mesa about eight miles north and slightly
west of Palm Springs and not far from Whitewater,
extending in fact nearly to the edge of Whitewater
Cañon. It is a natural cactus garden, where many
species of cacti are associated in what amounts to
a thicket of these odd vegetable forms. A trip to it
makes a pleasant cross-country horseback excursion; or it may be reached by automobile *via* the

Whitewater Ranch and the Morongo Pass road, say fifteen miles. (There are two bad sandy stretches of the road beyond Whitewater.) Time needed, about three hours horseback or one hour automobile each way.

The Garnet Hills are a ridge of gravelly ground just to the east of Palm Springs Station, which is about six miles due north of the village. The old sandy road to the east of the stage-road (a continuation of Indian Avenue) should be taken. There is nothing of special note here, but the place offers a convenient objective for a short horseback trip, as well as fine views of San Jacinto and San Bernardino Mountains and the open desert. Garnets are not hard to find, but none of good quality need be expected. Time needed, about two hours each way.

The Gordon Trail, or P. and P. (Palm and Pine) Trail, is a direct route to the mountain resort of Idyllwild on San Jacinto Mountain. It was built at the expense and through the public spirit of Mr. M. S. Gordon of Palm Springs. It leaves the Palm Cañon road at a point just beyond the Government Experiment Station, and climbs by steep but not excessive grades, reaching about 8000 feet at one spot. Water will first be found at "Avispas," 2000 feet (two hours), then at Tahquitz Creek, 6000 feet, which should be the noon stopping-place. Thereafter the trail is through virgin forest (two hours to the highest point, whence it drops abruptly to Idyllwild.) Thus the through trip may be made on horseback in one day. Magnificent panoramic views of the desert and the Salton Sea are obtained, and in late spring a great display of blossoming mountain plants—wild lilac, yucca, manzanita, etc. Time needed, twelve hours, allowing one hour's rest.

NOTE—It is unwise to make this trip alone, and a safe, trail-broke horse, well shod, is necessary.

A pleasant short round-trip may be arranged by taking the Gordon Trail as far as a point above Andreas Cañon giving a fine view of the palisade cliffs and the desert, returning thence by a trail which branches off to the left (south) and descends to the cañon, whence there is a road to Palm Springs. (See Andreas Cañon trip.)

Hidden Spring Cañon is a secluded spot in the foothills of the Orocopia Mountains. This entails a longish trip, the distance being about fifty miles. The route is down the valley by the main road as far as Mecca (thirty-eight miles), thence three miles east on the Blythe road, then two miles southeast following the Power-line, then north up the wash into the cañon (this is a hard pull for automobiles.) Splendid near outlooks over the Salton Sea are obtained, and the cañon is remarkable, resembling Painted Cañon in formation and coloring. It contains a score or so of palms, also a spring of fair water, to reach which one must crawl on hands and knees through a narrow passage-way. Owing to slow travel, this trip can best

be handled as an over-night-camp trip, though a
strenuous one-day will cover it.

REFER to "Salton Sea" and "Painted Cañon"
trips, in same general locality.

Magnesia Spring Cañon opens to the southwest
upon the main valley road near Frye's Well, about
twelve miles from Palm Springs, (being the next
cañon to the northwest of Deep Cañon.) It is quite
easy of access, the approach being sandy instead
of bouldery, but automobiles may find difficulty
after leaving the main road (at a point opposite
Frye's old house.)   At the narrows, about two
miles from the mouth, there are fine cliffs; also a
little water, not of the best quality, yet drinkable;
and a rock-bound pool large enough for a miniature swim.   In the upper cañon there are a number
of palms.   This cañon makes a pleasant objective
for a picnic, or for a one or two days' camping-
trip.

Mission Creek Cañon is a cañon of San Bernardino Mountain opening northwesterly to the
north of Painted Hill, which is about three miles
north of Whitewater Station.   The distance from
Palm Springs is about fifteen miles.   The route for
automobiles (twenty miles) is by way of Whitewater Ranch and the Morongo Pass road, keeping
to the west at the forks: on horseback one may take
the old sandy road to Palm Springs Station, continuing north by a road which skirts the Devil's
Garden (q. v.)   The cañon has some remarkable

rock colorings and formations, with evidences of
volcanic action.   There are two or three ranches
belonging to Indians and whites: also good and
abundant water. Time needed, one day by automobile: one night out by horseback.

   The Morongo Trip. I use this term to desig-
nate an excursion, of whatever length one likes, into
the mountains that face one looking across the
desert to the north and east from Palm Springs
(actually a spur of San Bernardino Mountain, but
locally known as the Morongos.)   The route for
automobiles is by way of Whitewater Ranch,
branching off thence to the road running northeast
to the Morongo Pass. This leads by way of Warren's
Ranch ("Chuckwarren's"), Warren's Wells, and
Coyote Holes, to the oasis of Twenty-nine Palms, on
the southern edge of the Mojave Desert. A worth-
while loop is made by turning south at the sign-
board (six miles beyond Warren's Wells) marked
"Keyes Ranch, Quail Springs," etc.: another sign-
board at the Keyes Ranch will direct you to Twenty-
nine Palms via Gold Park. A great variety of
desert scenery is thus met, including exceedingly
striking rock formations and those botanical curi-
osities, the Joshua trees, as well as fine views of the
great peaks, San Jacinto, San Gorgonio, and Santa
Rosa.   The trip may be prolonged from Twenty-
nine Palms into a circuit by way of Dale, Cottonwood Springs, Shafer's Well, and Mecca, near the
north shore of the Salton Sea, but inquiries should
be made as to the state of the roads before venturing

on this extension. Time needed, one day the round
trip by automobile to the Keyes Ranch or Twenty-
nine Palms, (the latter being 136 miles, round
trip.)

Murray Cañon is a picturesque cañon opening
westward just to the south of Andreas Cañon (q. v.)
It has many fine palms and some interesting rock
formations, and provides a convenient and agree-
able short trip or picnic place. There is a fair
automobile road leading into the cañon. A small
stream of fair water runs in winter and spring.

Painted Cañon or Red Cañon is a remarkable ravine in what are locally called the Mud Hills,
on the northeast side of the Coachella Valley. It
opens about five miles north from Mecca, and thus
is about forty-three miles from Palm Springs. The
features of the cañon are the brilliant coloring of
the walls in places, and the height and verticality of
the cliffs. The approach to the cañon, and its floor,
are sandy and likely to be troublesome for automobiles. A small flow of water may be found two or
three miles up, but this is not dependable. Time
needed, one day by automobile.

REFER to "Salton Sea" and "Hidden Spring
Cañon" trips, in same general locality.

Palm Cañon. This may well be termed the
most notable point of Our Araby's scenery, and it
has been not a little "written up" and pictured in
magazine and newspaper articles. It opens about
seven miles south of Palm Springs, at the very end

of the arm of desert into which Andreas and Murray Cañons also debouch. An automobile road runs to the mouth of the cañon, which is a rocky, winding ravine, strikingly picturesque, crowded with palms to the number of, probably, thousands. A good stream of water flows in the cañon, and greatly enhances its charm. So unique and beautiful is the place that plans are afoot for setting apart this cañon and some surrounding territory as a National Park or Monument.

The Salton Sea, of which much has been written, is really a great lake formed by the overflow of the Colorado River. As a geographical accident, so to speak, of some note it is worth a visit, as well as for its scenic features and for its interest as a purely desert lake and an example of geological phenomena. Its nearest point to Palm Springs is the northern shore, which is a mile or two from the town of Mecca, thirty-eight miles down the valley. Good camping-places by the "sea," with fair water, are at Fig-tree John Springs and Fish Springs, directions for which can be learned at Mecca. Time needed, one day by automobile.

REFER to "Hidden Spring Cañon" and "Painted Cañon" trips, in same general locality.

The Sand-Dunes A trip to the big dunes will be worth the visitor's while, either the high dunes six or eight miles directly northeast of Palm Springs or the wide expanse of smaller dunes which lie near and to the left of the road as one goes down the valley, say sixteen miles out. The view is memorable among these great sand-masses, which realize one's idea of Arabia and the Sahara. A picnic here will be a novelty. Needless to say, no water can be expected among the dunes. Time needed, one day horseback.

Seven Palms is a small natural oasis on the open desert, about seven miles north and a little east of Palm Springs. It makes a pleasant horseback trip (or walk in cool weather), and may be reached by taking the old sandy road to Palm Springs Station and thence by a trail skirting the north edge of the Garnet Hills; or it can easily be found by striking across country toward the northerly point of the big dunes, looking out for the palms which will be in sight before the railroad is passed. The attractions are the palms, which are charmingly grouped, and the fine views of the mountain peaks to the southwest and northwest. There is water in plenty, but of poor quality. Time needed, two hours horseback.

Snow Creek Cañon o p e n s to the southwest opposite Whitewater Station, and is easily reached by following the stage-road to that point, whence a plain road leads into the cañon. A good stream of water flows all the year, and fair trout-fishing may be had in it in the season. In a side cañon on the south of the main cañon near its mouth there is a group of palms which is interesting as marking the westerly limit of the tree's growth. A branch road on the south side of the cañon leads to Snow Creek Falls, which are worth visiting when much water is coming down. Time needed, one to two hours by automobile.

Tahquitz Cañon, (named for the evil spirit of the Cahuillas) is marked by a striking break in the mountain wall just to the south of Palm Springs. It is the favorite resort in the neighborhood of the village, the popular route being the foot-path along the bank of the Tahquitz ditch, which follows the base of the mountain. The main feature of interest for most people is the waterfall, which after heavy rains is quite impressive; but the rock scenery, the cacti, and the outlook from the cañon portals are all well worth notice. There are two trails worth exploring, an upper and a lower. Automobiles can take a road (fair) just south of the village going to the mouth of the cañon. Only the lower part, as far as the fall, is accessible without hard and even dangerous climbing.

Thousand Palm Cañon lies to the east and somewhat south of Palm Springs, being on the opposite side of the valley and opening into the foothills of the San Bernardino spur. It is hardly accessible by automobile, but provides a fine day's horseback trip by striking across country through the dunes, crossing the railroad at Edom and continuing east by a middling road. The cañon contains remarkable groves of palms. Water of fair quality has been developed and is found near the mouth. As the distance from Palm Springs is about fifteen miles, and the country not easy, the trip can best be taken as a one-night-out expedition, but it is not too much for a return the same day if an early start be made.

Two-Bunch Palms is a double group of palms picturesquely placed on a bench at the foot of the hills three or four miles north of Seven Palms. It can be reached by continuing north across country from that place (q. v.), being easily found by looking out for the palms, which soon come in sight. The spot commands fine views of the open desert and the mountains. There is a spring of good water. This makes an enjoyable all-day's horseback picnic trip, Seven Palms being taken on the way. Time needed, a good three hours each way.

The Vandeventer Trail starts from near the foot of Palm Cañon (a little to the east) and climbs to the high plateau known as Piñon Flat. It is a long trail of about twenty miles following roughly the dividing line between the outlying spurs of San Jacinto and Santa Rosa Mountains. About halfway of the trail is a spot called Little Paradise, which is practically the only place where camp can be made in this rough piece of country, also the only spot where one may rely on getting water (in a small *ciénaga*, or marsh, not easily found.) The trip to this point and return may be made on horseback in one long day.

AT TWO-BUNCH PALMS: MT. SAN GORGONIO IN THE DISTANCE

Whitewater Cañon opens to the north from Whitewater Station, which is nine miles by the stage-road from Palm Springs. It contains nothing of special interest, but there are a few palms, also good water, and fair trout-fishing may be found in the season if one goes far enough in the cañon, up which there is a road for a considerable distance. By making the trip on horseback, across country, other places may be taken *en route*, viz: Seven Palms and the Devil's Garden, which makes it well worth while. Time needed, one long day horseback.

N. B. As regards excursions involving crossing the open desert (for instance, the trips to Seven Palms, Thousand Palm Cañon, the Sand-dunes, the Devil's Garden, etc.) it is advisable to choose one's day with special reference to wind conditions. On days of strong wind it may easily prove that the pleasure is outweighed by the discomfort.

VI. FLORA AND FAUNA

A LARGE element in the attraction of Our Araby lies in the novelty of its animal and vegetable life. The former is a matter principally for naturalists, who find interest in noting the variations from type as regards habits, color, size, etc., wrought by special conditions among the mammals, birds, and reptiles of the desert. Yet one need not be a scientist in order to appreciate the humors of, for instance, the jolly little hairy-tailed desert mice who have chummed up with me by many a camp-fire, where they equally amused and amazed me by taking headers into the hot ashes at every opportunity, as though the thought of being baked alive was irresistible. This, too, is the place to enjoy the antics of that fine joker and gymnast, the road-runner, of whom strange tales are told, yet none too strange to seem credible to his admirers.

There would be little value to anyone in printing here a detailed list of the birds and animals found in our territory. Such a list would run into hundreds of items (of rats, mice, gophers, or lizards, for instance, many different kinds would need to be noted, as well as of sundry birds:) and without the aid of colored illustrations it would be all but worthless, even if lengthy descriptions and measurements were given. A brief enumeration of the birds, mammals, and reptiles is given below, regarding which it should be borne in mind that not only the immediate neighborhood of Palm Springs but also the cañons and higher ground within a radius of some miles is included in the territory covered. This information is drawn from two publications of the University of California, viz: "An Account of the Birds and Mammals of the San Jacinto Area of Southern California," by J. Grinnell and H. S. Swarth, and "The Reptiles of the San Jacinto Area of Southern California," by Sarah Rogers Atsatt: both published by the University of California Press, Berkeley, California. To these the reader who desires complete data is referred.

BIRDS

Bluebird, Western
Bush-tit
Buzzard (Turkey vulture)
Chat, Long-tailed
Coot (Mud-hen)
Dove, Mourning
Duck, two or three species
Eagle, Golden
Falcon, Prairie
Flycatcher, two or three
  species
Gnatcatcher, two species
Goldfinch, two or three
  species
Grosbeak, Black-headed
  and Blue
Hawk, several species
Heron, Night
Hummingbird, several species
Jay, Piñon and California
Lark, Horned

Ouzel (Dipper)
Owl, two or three species
Pewee, Western Wood
Phainopepla
Phoebe, Say and Black
Plover, Killdeer
Poor-will, Dusky
Quail, three species
Raven, Western
Roadrunner
Robin, Western
Shrike (Butcher-bird)
Snipe, Wilson
Sparrow, many species
Swallow, two or three species
Swift, White-throated
Thrasher, Leconte
Towhee, two or three species
Verdin
Vireo, two or three species
Warbler, several species

(CONTINUED)

Lark, Meadow
Linnet (House finch)
Mockingbird
Nighthawk, Texas
Oriole, two or three species

Woodpecker, Cactus and Red-
   shafted (Flicker)
Wren, two or three species
Yellowthroat, Western

NOTE:The California Condor, one of the greatest of flying
birds, has within only the last few years vanished from this
region.

MAMMALS

Bat, two or three species
Chipmunk, Antelope
Cottontail rabbit
Cougar (Panther, Puma,
   Mountain-lion)
Coyote
Deer, Mule
Fox, Kit and Gray
Gopher, two species
Ground-squirrel, two species
Jackrabbit

Kangaroo-rat, two or three
   species
Mouse, various species
Pocket-mouse, two or three
   species
Sheep (Bighorn)
Skunk, two species
Wildcat (Lynx)
Wood-rat, White-footed and
   Brown-footed

REPTILES

Lizards, various, including the Chuckwalla and Horned-toad.
Snakes: Garter, Gopher, Rattlesnake, Red-racer, Sidewinder.
Tortoise.

A much larger number of people are interested
in the desert plants, which offer the advantage of
being always on view, than in the animal life,
which must be studied under difficulties. Many of
the desert growths are strange enough to challenge
attention at first sight: others steal into one's notice
or affection by virtue of some quaintness or beauty
of blossom, or by some trait of the useful or un-
expected. Detailed descriptions of such are out of
the question here, nor would descriptions, without

expensive colored illustrations, be much to the
point. The best that is possible in this small book
is to transcribe from my larger volume, "California
Desert Trails," a fairly complete list of the desert
plants, the brief notes on which will serve to iden-
tify a good many of them. The "Western Wild
Flower Guide" of Mr. Charles F. Saunders (an
invaluable manual for anyone interested in California's wild flowers) and the "Field Book of Western Wild Flowers" of Miss Margaret Armstrong in
collaboration with J. Thornber, both of which are
illustrated, include a fair number of the noticeable
desert flowers, and will be found useful for
reference.

VII. NOTICEABLE PLANTS OF THE DESERT

Botanists must kindly overlook the lack of exactitude in these descriptions, which are necessarily brief and in which technical terms have purposely been wholly avoided.

It should be borne in mind that a number of plants may be met on the desert, especially about settlements or cultivated areas, that are not native there. A few of these, such as are most likely to come under observation, are included below. If there seem to be omissions in the following list, the explanation may be that the plants in question do not properly come under desert classification.

Abronia aurita. Sand Verbena (not really a verbena, but somewhat like that plant in its flowering.) A low, trailing, sticky, soft-stemmed plant, bearing close clusters of fragrant, rosy-purple flowers. Blooms in midspring.

Acacia greggii. Cat-claw, Uña de gato. A bush up to 10 feet high, crowded with small sharp thorns, common in cañons and on hillsides: often mistaken for a small mesquit, the leaves being like those of that tree but smaller. Flower a yellowish "spike" (resembling a pussy-willow catkin): fruit a pod, often curiously twisted. Blooms in early summer.

Adenostoma sparsifolium. Red-shank, Bastard cedar, Chamiso, Yerba del pasmo. A tall, fragrant bush with red, shreddy bark and fine, stringy foliage. Found in the mountains bordering the desert, not widely distributed. Flowers small, white, profuse. Blooms in late spring.

Agave deserti. Wild Century-plant, Maguey, Mescal. Leaves blue-gray, very large, succulent, with strong prickles on edges and a thorn at apex, starting from the ground. Flower-stalk 8 or 10 feet high, bearing many sets of clustered, yellow, bell-shaped flowers.

Common in parts of the desert mountains. Blooms in mid-spring.

Amsinckia spectabilis. Fiddle-head, Zacate gordo. A very common, small, hairy, slender-stemmed plant, with narrow leaves and small orange flowers on stalks that curl at the tip. Blooms in early and mid-spring.

Anemopsis californica. Yerba mansa. A low, rank-growing plant found only in damp places. Leaves large and coarse: flowers large, white, with protruding conical centre. Blooms in mid-spring.

Aphyllon cooperi. Cancer-root. A low, succulent plant, somewhat like a stalk of asparagus, bearing a number of small, purplish flowers. The plant is a parasite, growing on the roots of other plants. Not common. Blooms in late summer.

Argemone hispida. Thistle poppy, Cardo, Chicalote. A prickly, gray or bluish leafed, thistly-looking plant, 1 or 2 feet high, with large, fragile flowers, white with yellow centre. Blooms in mid- and late summer.

Aster orcuttii. A hardy-looking plant of the driest desert cañons, 1 to 2 feet high; rather rare. Leaves stiff and paper-like, with prickly-toothed edges: flowers large and handsome, of lavender rays with yellow centre. Blooms in early summer.

Astragalus coccineus. A low plant with almost white stem and leaves and handsome cardinal-red flowers. Found in the desert mountains, but rare. Blooms in mid-spring.

Atriplex canescens. Salt-bush, Shad-scale. A good-sized roundish bush with small, grayish leaves, inconspicuous flowers, and tassels of striking, bright green seed-vessels. Blooms in early summer.

Atriplex hymenelytra. Desert holly. A stiff, shrubby plant 1 or 2 feet high, with whitish, holly-like leaves and inconspicuous flowers. Found in alkaline soil in dry cañons or on open desert. Blooms in mid-spring.

Atriplex lentiformis. Quail-bush. A large gray bush very common on silt or alkaline soil, up to 15 feet high, and usually of smooth, dome-shaped outline. Flowers inconspicuous. Blooms in mid-spring.

Baileya pauciradiata. Cotton-plant. A small, loosely growing plant with pale gray-green stems, narrow woolly leaves, and small, lemon-yellow flowers. Blooms in mid- and late summer.

Bebbia juncea. A roundish, dark green bush a foot or two high, with many slender, almost leafless stems and numerous small, yellow, fragrant flowers. Blooms throughout summer.

Beloperone californica. Chuparosa. A good-sized bush, almost leafless, with purplish green, downy stems and handsome, dark red, tubular flowers. One of the earliest blooming desert plants, continuing all spring.

CACTI:—

Cereus engelmanni. Hedgehog cactus. A cluster of spiny short stems about the size and shape of cucumbers. Flowers very handsome, large, cup-shaped, bright rose-purple with plumy green stigma. Blooms in mid-spring.

Cereus giganteus. Saguaro, Pitahaya. The giant cactus, common on the Arizona desert hills and found sparingly in California adjacent to the Colorado River. It is a tall, fluted column up to 60 feet high, usually with similar vertical offsets for branches. Flowers large, white: fruit crimson, edible. Blooms in mid-spring.

Echinocactus cylindraceus. Barrel cactus, Nigger-head, Biznaga (or Viznaga). A large, cylindrical, ribbed cactus up to 6 feet high (globular when young) covered with long curving spines. Flowers greenish yellow, cup-shaped, in a circle on the top. Blooms in mid-spring.

Mamillaria tetrancistrus. Pincushion, Strawberry, or Fish-hook cactus, Chilito. A small, round cactus, usually 1 or 2 inches in height and diameter, with a fuzz of fine white spines and a longer sharply hooked black one in the centre of each tuft. Flowers fleshy, lily-like, of rich claret color: fruit scarlet, finger-shaped, edible. Blooms in late spring.

THE BIZNAGA, A STRANGE INHABITANT OF THE
GARDEN OF THE SUN

Mamillaria sp. Like a larger growth of the foregoing, but somewhat irregular in shape and with waxy-white flowers. Blooms in late spring.

Opuntia basilaris. A flat-lobed, grayish cactus, velvety-looking, without noticeable spines but set with myriads of minute prickles. Flowers very handsome, large, cup-shaped, cerise, set in row on edge of lobe. Blooms in mid-spring.

Opuntia bigelovii. Cholla. A plant up to 6 feet tall, branching in stumpy arms, the whole plant densely clad with greenish white spines. The older parts turn almost black. The joints detach very easily and litter the ground. Flowers greenish white. Blooms in mid- and late spring.

Opuntia chlorotica. Prickly pear, Indian fig, Nopal. The common flat-lobed cactus of the coast, found also on the desert mountains. Flowers pale yellow, sometimes with reddish tinge, set in a row on edge of lobe: fruit dark red, edible, but covered with fine prickles. Blooms in mid-spring.

Opuntia echinocarpa. Deer-horn cactus. A very branching cactus up to 5 feet high, the joints pale green, very spiny though less so than *O. bigelovii.* Flowers greenish with bronzed look outside. Blooms in mid-spring.

Opuntia ramosissima. Similar in habit to *O. echinocarpa* but with much slenderer stems and fewer but stronger spines. Flowers small, brown. Blooms in late spring.

Cassia armata. A low bushy plant with handsome yellow flowers, found in the desert mountains, but rare. Blooms in mid-spring.

Centaurea melitensis. Star thistle, Jocalote. A small, usually single-stemmed plant a foot or so high, with narrow gray-green leaves. Flowers small, yellow: flower-heads very prickly. Blooms in mid-spring and summer.

Cercidium torreyanum. Palo verde, Lluvia de oro. A tree up to 30 feet high, noticeable for the smooth green bark of the entire tree. Foliage small, scanty, and short-lived, so that the tree is usually bare: the twigs bear short thorns. Flowers profuse, bright yellow: fruit a pod. Blooms in mid-spring.

Chilopsis linearis. Desert willow (not properly a willow but belonging to the Bignonia family.) A small, willow-like tree, up to 20 feet high, usually found in washes. Leaves narrow: flowers handsome and plentiful, white marked with lilac and yellow, fragrant; fruit a pod, very long and narrow, remaining on the tree after the seeds have fallen. Blooms from mid-spring to autumn.

Chorizanthe brevicornu. A small, leafless, yellow-green plant, resembling the dry yellow moss sometimes found on pine trees. Flowers inconspicuous.

Coldenia plicata. A hardy-looking, mat-like plant with small, deeply-veined, dark green leaves and tiny white flowers. Blooms in mid-spring.

Croton californica. One of the commonest desert plants. A thin bush 2 or 3 feet high, with many slender straight stems and few light-gray oval leaves. The plant gathers into a goblet-shaped tuft as it dries. Flowers small, yellowish. Blooms from late spring to late summer.

Dalea:—the genus has been re-named Parosela, q. v.

Datura meteloides. Jimson weed, Tolguache (or Toluache). A rank-growing plant 2 or 3 feet high, common on both coast and desert, with large, coarse, dark-green leaves and very large, white or pale lilac, trumpet-shaped flowers that open in the evening. Blooms from spring to autumn.

Dithyrea californica. A small coarse-leafed plant found in sandy soil usually about bushes. Flowers small, fragrant, of four white petals. Blooms in early spring.

Encelia californica. A stiff, bushy plant with dark-green leaves and brittle, woody stems, common on and near the base of desert mountains. Flowers bright yellow,

on straight stalks that project well above the rest of
the plant. Blooms in mid-spring.

Encelia farinosa. Incense bush, White brittle bush, Yerba
de incienso. One of the commonest of desert plants in
the neighborhood of mountains, in form a compact
rounded bush 2 to 3 feet high. Leaves silver-gray,
firm in texture: flowers like those of *E. californica.*
The plant exudes drops of amber-colored gum. Blooms
in mid-spring.

Ephedra californica. Desert tea, Canutillo. A shrub 2 to
3 feet high, entirely composed of straight, smooth, dark-
green stems without leaves. Flowers inconspicuous.

Eremiastrum bellioides. Desert star. A small prostrate
plant, hardly noticeable except for its pretty, daisy-
like flowers, borne on radiating horizontal stems.
Blooms in mid-spring.

Eremocarya micrantha. A small, slender herb with small
linear leaves and tiny white flowers. It dries to a
whitish, woolly-looking little plant that is greedily
eaten by horses. The root yields a bright madder
stain. Blooms in early spring.

Eriodictyon tomentosum. Yerba santa. A bush 5 or 6 feet
high, found in cañons, with narrowish, gray-green,
woolly leaves and clusters of lavender funnel-shaped
flowers. (It is the coast species, *E. glutinosum,* or
E. californicum, with smooth, dark-green, sticky leaves,
that was so highly valued for its medicinal properties
by the Spanish Californians.) Blooms in late spring.

Eriogonum inflatum. Bottle plant, Desert trumpet. A plant
up to 3 feet high, with a few slender, straight, straggling stems that end in elongated swellings. Leaves
heart-shaped, growing only at base: flowers small,
yellowish. Blooms in mid-spring.

Eulobus californicus. A slender, straight, spindling plant,
a foot or so high, with small yellow flowers and very
narrow straight seed-vessels. Blooms in late spring.

Euphorbia polycarpa. Rattlesnake weed, Golondrina. A
flat-growing, mat-like plant with radiating reddish stems

and small, roundish, bronze-green, white-edged leaves. Flowers very small, white or pinkish. Blooms in late spring.

Fagonia californica. A low, open-growing plant found on rocky desert hillsides, with hardly noticeable leaves but many pretty, star-shaped, pale magenta flowers. Blooms in mid-spring.

FERNS:—These are naturally rare in desert regions, and are found only along the bases of the mountains, where falls the greater part of the little rain that occurs in this arid territory. Besides those named there are a few others which are very rarely found.

Cheilanthes viscida. Lip fern. Fronds elongated, dark green, very much dissected, and covered with a sticky secretion. Found usually in crevices of the rocks in cañons.

Notholaena cretacea. Cloak fern. Fronds triangular in outline, moderately divided, and thickly coated with a white powder. When dry they roll up into brittle balls, but when rain comes they unroll and resume life. This and the species next named usually grow under the edges of rocks and boulders on hillsides, or on the sides of cañons.

Notholaena parryi. Cloak fern. Fronds elongated, rather narrow, pinnately divided, the upper surface densely clothed with whitish hairs, the lower brown and woolly.

Fouquieria splendens. Candle wood, Ocotillo. A unique plant composed of a number of long gray thorny canes diverging at ground: usually 6 or 8 feet high but sometimes double as much or over. Leaves small, dark-green, and short-lived: flowers scarlet, tubular, in a long spike at ends of canes. Blooms in early spring, or at any time when sufficient rain has fallen.

Franseria dumosa. Burro-weed. A stiff, brittle, rounded, gray bush, common on and near the base of desert mountains. Leaves small, gray-green: flowers yellowish, in close spikes. The plant has a strong, somewhat turpentiny smell. Blooms in mid-spring.

GRASSES:—

Cynodon dactylon. Bermuda grass. Not properly a desert grass, but has become established in the irrigated areas. It is bright green and close-growing, with small, pointed leaves. It makes good emergency forage.

Distichlis spicata. Salt grass. A low-growing, pale green or gray grass, leaves in double rank, herring-bone style. It is very common, forming a close sod on moist, and especially on alkaline, soils. Animals will eat it when hard pressed.

Epicampes rigens. Basket grass, Zacaton. A tall, rigid, slender-stemmed, pale green grass forming large tussocks 2 to 4 feet high. It grows among rocks near streams, and on dry hills, and though poor fodder is valued by Indian women for basketry purposes.

Oryzopsis membranacea. Sand grass. A small, tussocky grass with slender stems 6 to 12 inches long, leaves bright green. It is found in sandy soil and makes good forage; also is valuable to the Indians for its edible seeds.

Panicum urvilleanum. A strong, coarse grass with rather stiff, pale green leaves a foot or more long. It grows in loose dry sand, and has little, if any, forage value.

Pleuraphis rigida. Blue-stem, Galleta. A coarse-, almost woody-stemmed, stiff grass growing in large dense clumps 2 to 4 feet high, and in the driest of soils. The stems appear dry and dead except at the tips, which are pale bluish green. It is an excellent forage-plant.

Sporobolus airoides. Zacaton. A coarse, stiff bunch-grass 2 or 3 feet high, flowering in loose, spreading panicles.

Tridens pulchella. A low, tufted grass 2 to 6 inches high, common on dry hills and mesas, often among rocks, with small dense panicles of blossom in which the tips of the flower-bracts are tinged with purple. It has practically no forage value.

Hesperocallis undulatus. Desert lily, Ajo. A true lily, with narrow, ribbony, crinkle-edged leaves lying flat at the base of the straight flower-stem, which is about 2 feet high. Flowers 3 or 4 inches in diameter, fragrant, white with green veining on back of petals, several to a stem. Blooms in mid-spring.

Hibiscus denudatus. A shrub 1 or 2 feet high, with scanty gray-green leaves and large, handsome flowers, white with dark purple "eye." Blooms in late spring.

Hoffmanseggia microphylla. A tall, loosely-growing plant found in dry desert cañons. Usually a number of the slender cane-like stems grow in a clump together. Leaves twice compound, of numerous minute leaflets: flowers yellow, in an open elongated cluster.

Hofmeisteria pluriseta. A small bushy plant growing in the crevices of rocky cliffs, the stems slender but woody, and the leaf-blades like a flattened tip on the leaf-stems. Flowers in small heads, abundant but not showy.

Hymenoclea salsola. Salt bush. A common, large, grayish bush with small, narrow leaves. Flowers very small, greenish, in profuse clusters at end of twigs. Blooms in late spring.

Hyptis emoryi. Lippia. A tall bush of the lower mountain slopes, up to 10 feet high, with rather straight stems usually branching from the ground. Leaves gray-green: flowers small, numerous, lavender colored, in loose spikes. The leaves and blossoms have a lavender-like smell. Blooms from mid-spring to autumn.

Isocoma acradenia. A small shrub with narrow, dark-green leaves and small, yellow flowers; common and widely distributed. Blooms in early spring.

Isomeris arborea. Bladder-pod. A vigorous, ill-smelling shrub 4 to 8 feet high, with light-green, triply-divided leaves and clusters of showy, yellow flowers. The seed-vessel is a large pale-green pod. Blooms from earliest to late spring.

Krameria parvifolia. A common bush of the lower mountain slopes, 2 feet or so high, with few, inconspicuous

leaves and purplish gray, much-interlaced stems and
twigs. Flowers deep claret color: seed-vessels small,
round, prickly. Blooms in mid- and late spring.

Larrea glandulosa. Creosote bush, Greasewood, Hediondía.
The commonest and most widely distributed shrub of
the desert, growing up to 12 feet high, in strong, somewhat brittle stems diverging from the ground. The
branches and twigs are regularly marked with rings.
Leaves small, glossy, bright dark green, sticky, with
strong tarry odor: flowers profuse, bright yellow, ma-
turing to small, round, woolly seed-vessels. Blooms from
mid-spring to mid-summer.

Lycium andersonii. A strong bush usually 4 or 5 feet high,
but in open desert a low patch of stiff intertangled
stems. Leaves small, gray: flowers few and small,
tubular, pale lilac: fruit a small, transparent, edible
(but insipid) red berry. Blooms in mid-spring.

Malvastrum rotundifolium. Five-spot. A small, upstanding,
hairy plant, often branching, with roundish leaves and
handsome cup- or globe-shaped flowers of pale lilac
with a carmine spot at base of each of the five petals.
Blooms in late spring.

Martynia proboscidea. Elephant's trunk, Devil's claw. A
rank, weedy plant, not common, with large, roundish
leaves and a few handsome flowers, white with yellow
and purple markings. The seed-vessels are dispropor-
tionately large, from 6 to 10 inches long, curved and
tapering, splitting as they dry into two long, springy
horns connected at base. Blooms in summer and into
autumn.

Mentzelia involucrata. A plant of the open desert, a foot
or more high, with thistly-looking, gray leaves and very
handsome, large, satiny flowers, white or creamy with
fine vermilion pencilling. Blooms in mid-spring.

Mirabilis aspera. A small, bushy plant with slender
branching stems and grayish leaves, found near the
base of mountains. Flowers white, primrose-like, opening at evening. Blooms in late spring.

Mohavea viscida. A small, hairy plant with straight, usually single stem and narrow leaves. Flowers large, deep cup-shaped, satiny, greenish-creamy with small purple dots: petals saw-edged. Blooms in mid-spring.

Nama demissum. A pretty little mat-like plant, sending out spoke-like arms at ends of which are small carmine flowers. Blooms in mid-spring.

Navarretia virgata. A small, dried-out looking plant of the open desert. Leaves inconspicuous: flowers numerous, pale bright blue. The last of the noticeable spring flowers, continuing into early summer.

Nicotiana bigelovii. Coyote tobacco. A many-stemmed plant, 1 to 2 feet high, with dark-green leaves and white, narrow-tubular flowers. Blooms midsummer to autumn.

Nolina parryi. A yucca-like plant of dry mountain-sides, not common. Leaves long, narrow, spiky, bluish green: flowers whitish, in a compact elongated cluster 2 or 3 feet long, on a tall stem rising from the centre of the sheaf of leaves. Blooms in mid-spring.

Oenothera gauraeflora. A small plant with straight, stiff, usually single stem bearing a cluster of small pinkish flowers. The bark is white and shreddy and the seed-vessels tongue-like and curved. Blooms in late spring.

Oenothera pallida. Sun-cups. A slender-stemmed plant with rather narrow, pointed and toothed leaves. Flowers bright yellow: seed-vessels curly with double twist. Blooms in mid- and late spring.

Oenothera scapoidea. A small plant with single stem 6 to 8 inches high, and a cluster of little pinkish flowers. One of the earliest spring flowers but blooms on into early summer.

Oenothera trichocalyx. Evening primrose. Yerba salada. A low, strong, rather spreading plant with large, rather narrow, grayish green leaves and very large fragrant flowers, white (pink when faded) with sulphur-yellow

THE OCOTILLO AND PALO VERDE

centres, opening at night. Blooms in mid- and late spring.

Olneya tesota. Ironwood, Palo fierro (or hierro.) A trim tree, up to 20 feet high, with thorny twigs and grayish green leaves composed of many leaflets. Flowers dull blue, like small pea-blossoms: fruit a pod. Blooms in early summer.

Palafoxia linearis. A common, straggling plant of many slender stems up to 3 feet high. Leaves few, narrow, dark gray-green: flowers lavender or pinkish, tubular, with long calyx. Blooms almost all the year.

Parosela (formerly Dalea) californica. A stiff, woody bush, up to 3 feet high, with clear yellowish bark. Leaves small, gray, narrowly divided: flowers plentiful, resembling pea-blossoms, dark, bright blue. Blooms in mid-spring.

Parosela (formerly Dalea) emoryi. Dye-weed. A gray, weedy bush 2 or 3 feet high, easily identified by the orange stain which the flower-heads leave on hands or clothing. Leaves small, composed of several leaflets: flowers tiny, purple, in small close clusters. Blooms mid-spring to late summer.

Parosela (formerly Dalea) mollis. A small, grayish plant with much-divided leaves and tiny, rosy-purple flowers in woolly-looking clusters. Blooms in late spring and early summer.

Parosela (formerly Dalea) schottii. A large, rather thorny bush, up to 6 feet high. Leaves very narrow, dark bright green: flowers resembling pea-blossoms, dark brilliant blue. Blooms in mid-spring.

Parosela (formerly Dalea) spinosa. Smoke-tree, Indigo-bush. A small tree, up to 15 feet high, common in washes. Practically leafless, the tree is a mass of whitish spiny twigs. Flowers small but very abundant, resembling pea-blossoms, dark brilliant blue. Blooms in early summer.

Pectis papposa. Chinch-weed. A low, small, rounded plant, vividly green, with bright yellow flowers. It has a strong, rather unpleasant smell. Blooms throughout summer.

Perityle emoryi. A small plant found growing among rocks. Flowers white, daisy-like. Blooms in mid-spring.

Petalonyx thurberi. Sandpaper-plant. A low, rounded, whitish bush with a peculiar roughness to the touch. Leaves small, light-green, scaly: flowers profuse, light yellowish green. Blooms in late spring.

Phacelia campanularia. Canterbury bell. A small, usually single-stemmed plant, with roundish, rather hairy leaves and large, deep-purple, bell-shaped flowers. Found (on the desert) only in cañons or near water. Blooms in mid-spring.

Phacelia sp. Wild heliotrope, Vervenía. A straggling, soft-stemmed, rather hairy plant, up to 4 feet high, with small, compound leaves and profuse, heliotrope-blue flowers in curling clusters. Blooms early to late spring.

Philibertia linearis. Twining milkweed. A strong creeper found on willows or other strong supporting plants, growing up to 6 or 8 feet high. Leaves few and grayish; flowers pale lavender, in a close rosette. Blooms in mid-spring.

Phoradendron californicum. Mistletoe. A parasite very common on the mesquit and other leguminous desert trees. It is leafless, but has numerous small pink or white berries.

Phragmites communis. Carrizo. A reed-like grass or cane, up to 10 feet high, with long, narrow leaves, found in damp places on the open desert.

Pluchea sericea. Arrowweed, Cachanilla. A straight-growing, cane-like plant, up to 10 feet high, abundant in damp places both in cañons and on open desert. Leaves gray, narrow, willow-shaped: flowers small, clustered, dull pinkish purple. Blooms in midsummer.

Prosopis glandulosa. Mesquit. A wide-branching, thorny tree, up to 20 feet high, found singly or in thickets. Leaves of many leaflets, resembling small leaves of the pepper-tree: flowers yellowish "spikes," (like pussywillows) : fruit long, narrow pods, in clusters. Blooms in late spring.

Prosopis pubescens. Screwbean mesquit, Tornillo. A smaller and slenderer tree than the foregoing, favoring alkaline soil. Leaves and flowers similar to the above, but somewhat smaller: fruit twisted pods, like screws, in clusters. Blooms in late spring.

Prunus eriogyna. Wild apricot. A large, branching, thorny bush, up to 8 feet high, found in some desert cañons. Leaves small, bright light green; flowers numerous, white, like small plum blossoms: fruit reddish yellow when ripe, with a small quantity of sweetish pulp. Blooms in early spring.

Psathyrotes ramosissima. A low, compact, rounded plant with light-gray leaves and small, yellow flowers. Blooms in late spring.

Purshia tridentata. Bitter-brush. A strong, woody bush 5 or 6 feet high, with a casual resemblance to the common creosote bush (*Larrea*) but rare. Flowers bright yellow. Blooms in late spring.

Rhus ovata. Sumac, Mangla. A large, compact, roundish bush or small tree, native to coast regions but sometimes found in or near desert cañons. Leaves dark bright green, glossy, suggesting those of the laurel: flowers white or pink, profuse, in very close clusters: fruit a reddish sticky berry. Blooms in late spring.

Salazaria mexicana. Bladder-bush. A roundish bush, up to 3 feet high, rather rare. Leaves few and small, gray: flowers showy, white and purple; the calyces become inflated and look like little round bladders. Blooms in early summer.

Salvia carduacea. Thistle-sage. A thistly-looking plant a foot or so high, with large, prickly, grayish leaves and handsome light-purple flowers in round-headed clusters. Blooms in late spring.

Salvia columbarieae. Chia. A small plant a foot or so high, usually with a single stiff stem rising from a

few deeply-cut leaves and bearing one or more clusters
of small purple flowers closely grouped in rings.
Blooms in mid-spring.

Sesbania macrocarpa. Wild hemp. A straight, slender,
spindling plant, up to 8 feet high, found in damp
ground in Imperial Valley and near the Colorado
River. Flowers yellow, pea-like. Blooms in mid- and
late summer.

Simmondsia californica. Goat-nut, Quinine-plant. A strong
shrub, up to 6 feet high, with gray-green leaves somewhat like those of the manzanita. Flowers whitish,
inconspicuous: fruit a small, brown, edible nut with
smooth, pointed husk. Blooms in mid-spring.

Sphaeralcea ambigua. Wild hollyhock. A loose-growing
plant, up to 3 feet high, with grayish stems and leaves.
Flowers numerous and striking, of a peculiar light-
vermilion color. Blooms in midspring and early summer.

Stephanomeria exigua. A low, slender-stemmed plant bearing a white starry flower something like that of the
single pink. Blooms in mid-spring.

Stillingia annua. A very small but hardy-looking plant with
stiff, saw-edged, light green, upright leaves. Flowers
inconspicuous.

Suaeda ramosissima. A common, loose-growing bush of the
open desert, 3 or 4 feet high, with very slender, bright-
green, juicy stems that give a pink stain on being
crushed. Leaves and flowers inconspicuous.

Trichoptilium incisum. A small, almost white plant, very
woolly, with small, composite, yellow flowers. Blooms
in early summer.

Washingtonia filifera. Fan palm. The native palm of the
desert, found in many cañons and occasionally in the
open desert, though never in dry soil. Up to 70 feet
high. Fronds light-green, with stringy filaments: flowers
small, creamy, in long, drooping clusters: fruit a small
hard berry, black and sweet when ripe. Blooms in
early summer.

Yucca brevifolia. Joshua tree, Yucca palm. A tree-yucca, up to 30 feet high, with stiff, strong arms and tufts of blade-like leaves, found in certain mountain and high mesa localities. Flowers whitish, bell-shaped, in large clusters, rather ill-smelling: fruit a short, thick pod which remains closed when mature and dry. Blooms in early spring.

Yucca mohavensis. A small tree-yucca, somewhat branching, with tufts of very long, dagger-like leaves, found in similar localities to those inhabited by the foregoing. Flowers also similar: fruit a large blunt pod which becomes soft and edible when ripe. Blooms in late spring.

Yucca whipplei. Spanish bayonet, Quijote. The common yucca of the coast mountains, with a very large spike of creamy, bell-shaped flowers on a tall, straight stalk rising from a sheaf of long, stiff, spiky leaves. Fruit becomes hard and splits open when ripe. Blooms in late spring.

VIII. CLIMATE AND HEALTH

EARLY one morning in April a few years ago a party of four, of whom I was one, were leaving Beaumont for Palm Springs. We had come from the coast, two of my friends driving in a camp-wagon, the other on horseback like myself. This was our fourth day out.

The weather was cold and cloudy as we left Beaumont, and a dash of rain spattered us as we raced through Banning, six miles on our road. It looked as if more were coming, so we who were on horseback halted a moment on the edge of town and put our ponchos on. From here we had a twelve mile straight-away stretch down to the Whitewater Ranch. The clouds hung heavy and low on the great mountains to right and left, and at our two thousand feet of altitude we looked out from under the stormy canopy as from beneath a hood. The effect was highly theatrical. Below and far ahead, at the foot of the hollow scoop of the pass, lay a pale golden land, shimmering in sunlight under a sky of summery blue. It was like magic, or a dream, and we gazed with all our eyes: but on the moment an icy blast rushed down from Grayback and lashed us with a storm of hail. This, anyhow, was no dream. Hastily we mounted and dashed forward; but for an hour as we galloped down the pass we were alternately thrashed on the

back with chilly rain and pelted liberally with
hail: while all the time the golden land stretched
away before us, smiling lazily in the sun. Suddenly,
a mile or two below Cabezon, we rode out into
glorious warmth. The rest was pure enjoyment.
We lunched in pleasant shade of a desert willow at
Whitewater Point and by early afternoon were at
Palm Springs receiving a good Scots welcome from
our old friend Doctor Murray. That night we
stretched out luxuriously under the flowering gre-
villeas of the Brooks House, bathed in moonbeams
and odor of orange-blossoms, lulled by the soft
clatter of palm-fronds and an occasional somnam-
bulistic outbreak from the night-herons roosting in
the cottonwoods near the spring.

I have related this by way of illustration. It is
an incident which could be duplicated a score of
times any winter or spring. Day after day we residents and visitors of Our Araby may sit snugly in
the sun, watching, like a show, the gloomy or angry
moods of the Cloud King in his mountain fastnesses
over San Bernardino, San Jacinto, and Santa Rosa,
and rubbing our hands over the contrast. Night
after night we may lie out under a full hemisphere
of stars, breathing air which Professor Van Dyke
properly names "the finest air on the continent,"
with no thought of rheumatic or neuralgic imps
lurking in fog or dew. Morning after morning we
may wake to see San Jacinto's flank of dusky red
turn suddenly to a mystery of rosy loveliness as the
sun flashes up over the eastern wall of the valley

—a thing which, though experienced a thousand times, I can never see without a feeling of being enchanted, or about to turn into a Maxfield Parrish.

But now to be more specific, for I wish to guard against the danger that lurks in "glittering generalities." Figures, as regards climate, do not tell everything, but they serve for a skeleton, and Government statistics are reliable, if nothing else. Here, then, are the U. S. Department of Agriculture's records of rainfall and temperature for a recent series of years: (the official figures for the succeeding years are incomplete.) The data are for Palm Springs Station, six miles from the village, and therefore are not exact for the latter point: but they will serve fairly.

AVERAGE MONTHLY TEMPERATURES AT PALM SPRINGS
STATION, YEARS 1907 TO 1915 INCLUSIVE

	Jan.	Feb.	March	Apl.	May	June	July	Aug.	Sept.	Oct.	Nov.	Dec.
Highest.	77	80	90	96	104	112	113	112	107	98	87	76
Lowest..	31	37	45	52	56	64	73	73	67	55	42	33
Mean...	53	55	63	69	73	84	90	90	84	73	62	52

In the nine years the maximum temperature reached was 118°, in July '07 and May '10. The minimum was 18°, which was touched in a "record" cold spell in January '13: with that exception 26°, in December '11, is the lowest figure for the nine-year period, with 28° on three occasions for next lowest.

RAINFALL, inches:
1907, 4.80; '08, 3.50; '09, 5.50; '10, 3.94; '11, 4.83; '12, 5.66; '13, 3.88; '14, 7.87; '15, 5.71.
(Average for the nine years, 5.08 inches.)

It will be seen that Palm Springs' average annual rainfall is about five inches, which, small as it is,

A SHADY LANE AT PALM SPRINGS

considerably exceeds that of localities only a few miles away on the open desert. Heavy falls of rain and snow occur on the mountain which rises close behind us, and we come in for the fringe of these storms: besides which, the mountain acts as our trustee in general, collecting our winter income of moisture and dealing it out to us as we need it by means of the Chino and Tahquitz Cañon streams. (The village draws also on San Bernardino Mountain for part of its water-supply, which is brought many miles across the desert from Whitewater Creek.) Thus it arises that along with a sufficiency of water (excellent water, too) our normal climate is the dry, sunny climate of the desert.

A remarkable range of temperature will be noticed in the figures given above—a natural feature of desert climates everywhere. (Even sleet has been seen at Palm Springs, but such a thing occurs only "once in a blue moon.") These wide variations occur not only between summer and winter but also between day and night temperatures, the explanation being, of course, the low rate of humidity (averaging 15 degrees) which is the usual condition. Through this dry air the sun's rays strike with a direct heat like that of a furnace, which, even when scorching, is never debilitating: and the moment the sun drops, the thermometer drops sharply with it. This gives us a conjunction of warm days with cool or even cold nights, and renders life, and even physical exertion, on the desert quite tolerable even in the heat of summer. Radia-

here, especially for lung and kidney affections. As regards tubercular patients, it should be noted that at the time of writing there is no proper accommodation available, so that it is very inadvisable for such persons to come to Palm Springs unless arrangements have been made for quarters. It is hoped that before long the needs of this class of health-seekers will be provided for.

Good results have been found to follow the use of the water of the hot spring, both for bathing and drinking, in cases of kidney disease. Further, it would be hard to find better conditions than those reigning at Palm Springs for the cure or help of nerve ailments; and here, if anywhere, the factors of pure air, sunshine, quietude, and healthful surroundings in general may be counted on by those seeking to regain or reinforce their health.

Subjoined is the Government analysis of the water of the spring.

	Milligrams per Liter
Metaboric Acid (BO2)	trace
Silica (SiO2)	44.8
Sulphuric Acid (So4)	37.3
Carbonic Acid (Co3)	33.0
Bicarbonic Acid (HCO3)	36.6
Nitric Acid (NO3)	0.1
Chlorin (CL)	25.0
Iron (Fe)	1.9
Calcium (Ca)	2.5
Magnesium (Mg)	0.7
Sodium (Na)	67.5
	249.4

Hypothetical Combinations

Sodium Nitrate (NaN03)	0.2
Sodium Chloride (NACL)	41.2
Sodium Sulphate (Na2S04)	55.2
Sodium Carbonate (Na2C03)	58.3
Sodium Bicarbonate (NaHC03)	29.4
Magnesium Bicarbonate (Mg(HC03)2)	4.2
Calcium Bicarbonate (Ca(HC03)2)	10.1
Ferrous Bicarbonate (Fe(HC03)2)	6.0
Silica (Si02)	44.8
	249.4

Temperature—104°

Since this book was printed a group of pleasant small cottages has been built for the accommodation of persons suffering from tuberculosis; but only early or arrested cases can be received. Application should be made by letter, in advance, to J. J. Kocher, M. D., Palm Springs, California.

IX. ACCOMMODATION AND CONVENIENCES, AND HOW TO COME

THOUGH Palm Springs is strong for simplicity our visitors need fear no hardships: indeed, our leading hotel is apt to prove a surprise to guests who come with the thought of "putting up with things." It is not the intention of the writer to advertise any of the business concerns of Palm Springs; but for the information of intending visitors it should be said that the best accommodation is offered by the Desert Inn, while less expensive quarters may be found at one or two other places in the village. A number of pleasant small tent-houses are rented by Mrs. L. F. Crocker, and these again are supplemented by a few others scattered about. Inquiries regarding quarters addressed to the Postmaster would be handed by him to the person most likely to be able to suit the applicant. Now and then one of the residents is willing to rent his or her comfortable house: in this case also the Postmaster would act as intermediary.*

As for "modern conveniences"—almost the only item in that ever-growing category that is a genuine

---

*As stated under *Climate and Health*, there are at present no regular arrangements for the accommodation of tubercular cases. Such should not come without quarters having been secured in advance.

necessity, viz., a piped water-system, Palm Springs possesses: the next in value, electric lighting, may shortly be expected to arrive. As yet we are free of the everlasting jingle of the telephone, yet have the really useful telegraph at command. Daily train service both east and west, with its corollary of daily mail and news service, need hardly be specified: they may be taken for granted.

To conclude: we are well served with stores: possess a neat church, nominally Presbyterian, in which services are regularly held (there is also a Roman Catholic church on the Indian Reservation): our school is creditable: we are furnished with the indispensable garage, well appointed: and the services of an excellent physician are always at our disposal except during the very hot months of the year, when the white population is practically *nil*.

*   *   *   *   *   *

Travelers coming BY TRAIN should buy tickets not to Palm Springs, but to WHITEWATER, which is the station at which the auto-stage meets the train. (Palm Springs Station is connected with the village only by a very poor road, not available for auto travel.) The distance to the village is nine miles, which is covered in half an hour. BY ROAD the route from the coast is via Pomona, Ontario, Riverside or San Bernardino, Beaumont, Banning, and the main desert road through Cabezon and Whitewater.

FOR MAIL the proper address is Palm Springs, Riverside County, California.

TELEGRAMS take the same address.

EXPRESS packages and FREIGHT should be addressed—Palm Springs via Whitewater, California.

APPENDIX

HINTS TO MOTORISTS

[Quoted by permission of United States Geological Survey from "Suggestions to Travellers" in Water-Supply Paper 490—A., "Routes to Desert Watering Places in the Salton Sea Region, California," by John S. Brown: Washington, 1920.]

More people travel the desert now in automobiles than in any other way, although horses are not unknown and even foot travellers are sometimes seen. Low-geared trucks with large tires have an advantage in freighting or traveling very sandy roads. With an experienced desert driver the average car can travel almost any road that is passable for wagons. Without careful driving it may fail to get anywhere on a comparatively good road. Automobile parties should always carry a supply of spare tires and tubes. A vulcanizing outfit for making patches is especially desirable. A tire gauge is very useful, and an air pump and a jack are necessary.

Sand is the worst obstacle . . . Fortunately it is less prevalent than popular fancy imagines. The average road consists of a pair of wheel ruts; and in sandy places it is essential to stay in these ruts. Leave them only to pass another vehicle and then keep two wheels of the car in a rut if the sand is bad. Parties attempting to pass on a sandy road can usually do so by helping push the autos if other means fail. Wheel ruts, if fresh, are easily traversed even in deep sand, but old ruts or wagon tracks make very difficult travelling for automobiles. On such roads if a car gets stuck it is often possible to back up and by getting a fresh start in one's own tracks break the road ahead through bad sand. A shovel is sometimes useful in short stretches for cleaning out covered ruts.

It is common practice in case of trouble in sand to deflate the tires. This gives the tire a greater bearing surface by allowing it to flatten out and increases the effectiveness of a car's gearing by reducing the diameter of the wheel. There is danger of rim cutting by having the tires too soft;

so that no more air should be allowed to escape than is absolutely necessary. No fixed rule is known, but for Ford cars a pressure of 35 or even 30 pounds was found safe and always gave good results. Tires are not damaged by running "soft" in sand, but they should be immediately pumped up when hard ground is reached, or they will suffer rim cuts, stone bruises, or blow-outs. The tire gauge is a necessity for judging the safe reduction of air pressure.

One great trouble in soft sand is that the wheels lose traction and spin, digging down and down into the sand. This is frequently brought about by attempting to start too suddenly. On the other hand, going too slowly when moving induces the wheels to spin. After a wheel has "dug in" it has to be "dug out" with a shovel, jacked up, and the hole surfaced with brush, canvas, or stones to give a bearing. Very effective use can be made of two strips of heavy canvas, say 30 feet long and 18 inches wide, for such difficulties. The strips must be thrust under the rear wheel, then laid lengthwise ahead in the ruts, and it is necessary to lift the front wheels and set them on the canvas to hold it down while the rear wheels pull. Otherwise the canvas is chewed up and "spit" out in the rear by the spinning wheels. Canvas solved the trouble of the worst sand for the Survey party without much recourse to brush or shovelling. Progress is slow, but nearly any bad place may be crossed in this manner. The use of canvas for occasional trips on well-travelled roads is seldom necessary. Most travellers, instead of using canvas, fill the ruts with broken twigs, brush, stones, or anything else available when they get stuck, but unfortunately the brush is usually thinnest where the sand is thickest. There are various devices on the market for pulling out automobiles which get stuck, and one of these may be a valuable part of the equipment. . . . .

. . . . A surplus of water over probable needs of men and automobiles should be provided. Oil and gasoline more than enough for probable needs should be taken, and it should be remembered that desert roads may require twice as much per mile as pavement.

PENCIL MEMORANDA